ZARA &
DAISY'S
JOURNEY

Once upon a time, in a vibrant meadow, lived Zara the Zebra and Daisy the Donkey. Both had traveled from far-off lands, having been separated from their mothers at a young age. Although they cherished their beautiful memories, they often experienced a deep longing for a place where they could truly feel at home — somewhere they could create new memories together.

One sunny day, as the two friends gathered in the meadow, they began to share their dreams and aspirations.

"What if we could find a place filled with friendship, laughter, and love?" Daisy proposed.

Zara's eyes lit up with excitement. "Yes! Let's embark on an adventure to discover a farm where we can belong!

With a renewed sense of purpose, Zara and Daisy set off on their journey, eager to uncover a place where they could thrive and build their own family. Together, they embraced the unknown, ready to explore the possibilities that lay ahead.

As they walked along the winding path that meandered through the forest, they admired the vibrant flowers bobbing in the wind and listened to the cheerful songs of birds overhead.

"I can't wait to see the farm and meet new friends!" exclaimed Zara, her ears perked up in excitement."

With hopeful hearts and a sense of wonder, Zara and Daisy packed a small bundle of essentials and set off into the forest. The path was unfamiliar, but their bond made every step feel lighter.

They laughed at rustling leaves and sang with the birds, their hooves creating a rhythm of joy on the forest floor.

As they ventured deeper into the woods, they met Benny the Bunny, who peeked out from behind a fern.

"Hello there," Benny greeted. "Where are you two headed?"

"We're searching for a place to belong," said Zara.

"Well," said Benny, "belonging begins in the heart. Want to hop along for a bit?"

And just like that, Benny joined their journey.

A little farther down the path, they found a patch of wildflowers.

"Let's make flower crowns!" Benny cheered.

"These will be our adventure crowns!" declared Daisy, placing a crown on Zara's head before fashioning one for herself.

Zara and Daisy giggled as they wove blossoms into each other's manes. The meadow echoed with laughter as their crowns shimmered in the sun.

"Now we're officially adventure royalty," Daisy declared.

With crowns on their heads and joy in their hearts, the trio danced through the meadow.

They twirled and leapt, feeling the wind in their fur and the magic of the moment. A squirrel clapped from a nearby tree, and even the flowers seemed to sway to their rhythm.

Their journey soon led them to the edge of a sparkling sea. Waves lapped at the shore as Delilah the Dolphin leapt from the water.

"Welcome, travelers!"
She chirped. "Come play!"

Zara stepped back, unsure.
"I don't know how to swim..."

Delilah smiled gently.
"Then today, you'll learn."

Delilah taught Zara to float, and Daisy to splash. Benny giggled as he balanced on a driftwood raft.

"Working together, we can make the biggest waves!" she exclaimed, showing them how teamwork could turn a simple moment into something magical.

They played in the waves, discovering that courage didn't mean being unafraid—it meant trying anyway, especially when friends were by your side.

Back on land, they dried in the sun and continued their journey. In the golden light of dusk, they stumbled upon a quiet glade where Eloise the Elephant was watering a garden with her trunk.

"Peace lives here," she said softly. "Would you like some water and rest?"

"Empathy strengthens our connections," she advised gently.

They nodded, grateful for her kindness.

As stars appeared in the night sky, an old oak tree rustled. Out peered Oliver the Owl.

"Travelers, remember this: wisdom isn't in knowing everything—it's in listening with your whole heart."

"Wisdom comes from reflection," Oliver hooted softly.

They sat in silence, watching fireflies dance as Oliver's words nestled deep into their hearts.

The next morning, the group met Timothy the Turtle, slowly making his way along the path.

"Life's not a race," Timothy said. "Sometimes the most important things take time."

"Sometimes, the best things take time," he advised, his voice calm and soothing.

They walked beside him, slowing their pace, and noticed so many little wonders they might've missed before.

As they meandered, they noticed birds collecting twigs, building a nest in perfect harmony.

"Even the tiniest ones work together," said Zara.

Their hearts swelled with the beauty of community and how every creature had a role to play.

Soon, they came across Fiona the Fox, who sat with a sparkle in her eye.

"To find your way," she said, "answer this riddle: What has keys but can't open locks?"

They pondered until Daisy whispered, "Love."

Fiona beamed. "A piano!"

Fiona beamed. "That's the answer. And the secret to home."

A butterfly fluttered past and landed on Zara's nose. Her name was Bella.

"I used to be afraid to change," Bella said. "But transformation is part of the journey."

As she flew off, the friends watched in awe, inspired by her gentle courage.

As Bella the butterfly fluttered ahead, guiding Zara and Daisy, they continued their journey toward the farm.

Along the way, they encountered Scout, a playful dog who eagerly joined their adventure. His enthusiasm was contagious, and together they trotted along the path, sharing stories and laughter.

Not far from there, they came across Kendall, a curious cat basking in a patch of sunlight beneath a tree. Intrigued by the lively group, Kendall decided to join them, adding a touch of curiosity to their travels.

"We've been waiting for you!" they said.

Scout wagged his tail and Kendall purred. "Your story isn't over—it's just beginning."

The group followed the winding road until a cozy little farm appeared in the distance.

It had a red barn, a flower-lined fence, and the soft sounds of animals welcoming them.

Zara and Daisy looked at each other, tears of joy sparkling in their eyes.

"We're home," they whispered together.

Under a tall tree, the friends
gathered in a circle.

They shared what they had learned:
about love, courage, transformation,
and the joy of belonging.

The breeze carried their laughter as
the sun painted everything gold.

Zara and Daisy looked around at their new friends, their new home, and their full hearts.

They had set out searching for belonging—and found it not just in a place, but in the journey, and in each other.

Zara and Daisy looked around at their new friends, their new home, and their full hearts.

They had set out searching for belonging—and found it not just in a place, but in the journey, and in each other.

And so, surrounded by those they loved, Zara and Daisy took one final step onto the path ahead.

Together, they walked toward the horizon, ready for whatever came next.

Because home... is where love walks beside you.

They remembered Benny the rabbit, who had taught them to embrace their uniqueness their stripes, their floppy ears, their differences and to find joy in simply being themselves. The more they accepted who they were, the more lightness they carried into each new day.

Whenever fear or sadness visited, they recalled
Eloise the elephant's gentle wisdom
that emotions are not to be avoided, but
honored. Together, they learned to sit with their
feelings, knowing that even hard emotions were
part of becoming stronger and more whole.

Timothy the turtle's steady pace reminded them to slow down and trust the timing of their own growth. On days when life felt uncertain, they would pause under the tall trees, breathing deeply, allowing space for healing to gently unfold.

They practiced creativity like Fiona the fox,
finding small, joyful ways to care for themselves
Whether through playful games, peaceful walks,
or simple moments of stillness. They discovered
that nurturing their inner world brought peace
to the world around them.

The wise owl, Oliver, had gently encouraged them to listen to their hearts. As seasons changed, Zara and Daisy became more attuned to their own needs learning when to rest, when to play, when to ask for help, and when to stand strong.

And whenever change felt uncomfortable, they remembered Bella the butterfly, who had once been small and unsure too. Bella's shimmering wings whispered to them, "Growth may feel uncertain, but beautiful things await on the other side."

Every friend they met along the way had offered them a gift — and together, these lessons created a life filled with self-love, compassion, and a sense of belonging.

As time passed, Zara and Daisy shared these lessons with the other animals on the farm. The farm blossomed into a place where everyone — young and old — could feel safe to express their feelings, honor their uniqueness, and support one another through every season of life.

And in doing so, they didn't just build a home
— they built a community where healing, joy,
and love could grow.

As their story comes to a close, Zara and Daisy's journey reminds us all that self-love, emotional awareness, and kindness toward ourselves and others can create the most beautiful kind of home — one we carry within us, wherever life may lead.

EPILOGUE

Zara and Daisy's journey reminds us that home isn't just a place
it's the love we carry within us, wherever life may lead.

Today, the real Zara the zebra and Daisy the donkey still live together
at our sanctuary in the mountains of North Carolina. They spend their
days grazing in the sun, sharing quiet moments under the trees, and
reminding us of the beauty of friendship, resilience, and belonging.

A portion of the profits from this book helps care for Zara, Daisy, and
their friends at the sanctuary, so their story — and the lessons they
share — can continue to inspire children and families everywhere.

From my heart to yours thank you for walking this journey with us.

Nicole Mescia (Solena Grace)

If we can have change or energy and you change your life.

~ Dr Joe Dispenza

authornicolemescia.com
@arisewithnicole
@maplehillfarm828

MORE TO EXPLORE

Thank you for joining Zara and Daisy's journey. To learn more about the real-life sanctuary that inspired this story — and the animals who still live there

visit: authornicolemescia.com
Instagram: @arisewithnicole
@maplehillfarm828

COLORING
PAGES

www.ingramcontent.com/pod-product-compliance
Lightning Source LLC
LaVergne TN
LVHW010028070426
835513LV00001B/22